KU-168-282

Turkey? Hungary? Tell me Max, are you thinking about your tummy?

Yes.

Then you are in luck because we're heading to the province of Ulster, home to the famous Ulster Fry!

Ulster

Imagine a big plate of sausages, bacon, eggs...and some special kinds of fried bread!

Isn't that unhealthy?

Only if you eat them all the time...everything in moderation my dear Molly!

I WANT AN ULSTER FRY!

Well, get out the Ulster map and see if you can find a place that makes them!

But maps are a puzzle to me!

Giant's Causeway

Carrick-a-Rede Rope Bridge

Dunluce Castle

Glens of Antrim

H & W

Springhill House

Lough Neagh

Belfast Zoo

Ulster Museum

Carrickfergus Castle

Harland and Wolff Shipyard

Lough Neagh Discovery Centre

Titanic Belfast

Folk & Transport Museum

Strangford Lough

Mourne Mountains

Down Cathedral

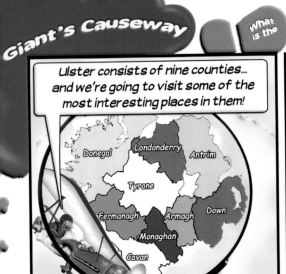

What is the biggest number you can write down & say?

Ulster consists of nine counties... and we're going to visit some of the most interesting places in them!

Donegal

Londonderry

Antrim

Tyrone

Fermanagh

Armagh

Down

Monaghan

Cavan

That's after I get an Ulster Fry, right?

Well Max, I was thinking that we start with an Ulster boil.

What does that mean Mick?

We'll get to that Molly, but first there's something you need to know about this little plane of ours.

IF1

It's also a time machine!

TIME TUNNEL

Really...does that mean we can fast forward through all this talking and get to the eating?

I'm afraid not Max because we're going the other way...sixty-five million years back in time!

A million has six zeroes.

8

Giant's Causeway, County Antrim

Giant's Causeway, County Antrim

You'll notice all these hexagonal rock patterns that were formed when the lava cooled in a certain way.

Hexagonal means that it has six sides!

The only sides I'm interested in at the minute are sides of bacon!

Well Max, if these facts about the Giant's Causeway don't interest you, then maybe a story would.

A story! A story! I want to hear a story!

11

If we roll back through the mists of time, we might stumble upon a tall tale...

Sixteen metres tall in fact, which was the height of a giant named Finn MacCool!

Now as giants go, Finn wasn't that big...not compared to Benandonner.

...Finn's rival who lived across the sea in Scotland!

One day, as Finn wandered along the Ulster coast, he heard Benandonner hurl insults at him!

This angered him so much that he hurled a rock back!

Benandonner said that Finn was weak and if he could cross the sea he'd show the Irish giant what true strength was!

Enraged, Finn started to rip columns of rock from the cliffs.

...And tossed them into the water!

Day and night he worked for a week.

Until he'd built a path all the way to Scotland so Benandonner could cross.

...And cross he did.

Suddenly, the Irish giant saw his rival for the first time...HE WAS HUGE!

Finn would never match Benandonner, so he ran all the way home.

...And told the whole story to his wife, Oonagh.

Now, Oonagh was a clever woman and she quickly came up with a plan.

She made Finn dress up as a baby.

Just as Benandonner barged in and demanded to see the Irish giant.

15

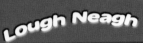

Finn seemed to throw quite a few things at Benandonner.

There's also a story of him scooping a huge lump of earth out of the ground and tossing it at the Scottish giant!

It didn't quite reach and crashed into the Irish Sea!

This piece of land became known as the Isle of Man.

Ulster

Isle Of Man

...And the hole left in Ulster filled with water to become Lough Neagh.

Lough Neagh

It is the largest lake in Britain and Ireland.

With plenty of places to explore along its shoreline, such as Lough Neagh Discovery Centre.

Lough Neagh

19

What year do you think

your parents were born?

Or your grand-parents?

What does BC and AD mean?

I'm not sure when giants roamed Ulster, but normal sized men came along in about 8000BC.

Here at Navan Fort, tools and pots have been found from about 4000BC.

Navan Fort, County Armagh© NIEA

They found pots? Perhaps I could cook my own Ulster Fry!

From around 600BC a tribe called the Celts settled in Ireland.

Here's a funny fact: Celtic gangs tried to scare their foes by charging into war naked!

Which must have made for some strange battlefields.

...Because these gangs, or clans, spent a lot of time fighting each other for power and land!

This led to clan leaders, or chieftains, carving Ireland up and claiming to be king of their own areas.

20

Of course, the ultimate goal for each king was to have all the others bow to him and so become High King of Ireland!

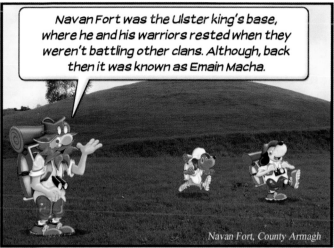

Navan Fort was the Ulster king's base, where he and his warriors rested when they weren't battling other clans. Although, back then it was known as Emain Macha.

Navan Fort, County Armagh

At Emain Macha, you'd find pagan worship.

BACON WORSHIP?

No Max, he said PAGAN, it was an ancient religion full of strange gods.

They had gods for everything; the sky and sun, birth, death, love, war, water, fire, food...

The pagans would worship these gods by offering up gifts ...including human sacrifices!

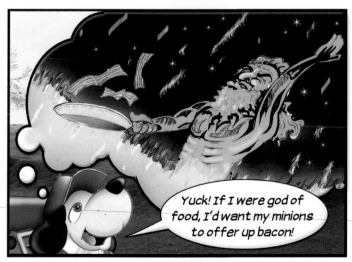

Yuck! If I were god of food, I'd want my minions to offer up bacon!

If you pay a visit to the nearby Navan Centre, you can learn all about the Celts and hear fantastic tales of myth and legend, like this one...

The low morning sun was only just beginning to burn off the frosty dew as young Setanta began his journey north, to Emain Macha and the lands ruled by his uncle, King Conor. For as long as he could remember, huddled around the fire on cold winter evenings, the little boy had listened to tales of King Conor. He'd heard of the army of boys who played hurling in the field every day, watched by the king and his fiercest warriors, and was determined to join them so that he could show off his skills.

Setanta's mother was far from happy that her son, at barely six years of age, should make the trip alone. However, as the king's only sister, she knew that her brother would look after the boy when he arrived.

On his journey, Setanta brought all of his favourite playthings; a ball made of silver, his hurley stick of bronze, a leather shield and a long blackthorn staff with a sharp point, hardened by flames.

Whistling merrily as he made his way along the grassy tracks, Setanta passed the time by batting his ball high into the air, then throwing his hurley stick after it. The stick would hit the ball in mid-air sending it even further. He would then fling his staff after both of them, running to catch all three before they hit the path. This game continued for hours and not once did the boy let any of them touch the ground.

Finally, as the shadows in the late afternoon sun grew longer, Setanta came to the top of a hill and looked down on Conor's kingdom. Far below a large group of boys practised their hurling skills on a grassy field in front of a cluster of huge stone houses. Men sat at large flat rocks outside these houses, playing chess and watching the boys hit balls to and fro.

Setanta raced down the hill and immediately began to show great skill with his own hurley stick. He stole a ball from the feet of Folloman, who also happened to be the king's son, and battered it hard towards a goal at one end of the field. Again and again he did this until the balls from all one hundred and fifty boys had been driven into the same net!

Furious, the boys gathered up their balls and with a crescendo of almighty thumps, they hit them towards Setanta who stood at the other end of the field. The fearless young lad flicked his stick from side to side, easily deflecting each one so that not a single ball passed by him into his goal. This enraged Folloman and, as leader of the boys, he howled at his troop to attack! Setanta never flinched as fifty of them, all screeching like banshees, ran down the pitch.

As the first wave towered over him, ready to crash down, Setanta let out a gut-wrenching roar and dived straight in. With a wild frenzy of fists and feet Setanta struggled against the tide until, when finally he stood, there was a gentle sea of boys all rolling in pain on the ground.

On witnessing this, the rest of the troop scattered and sprinted for the safety of the stone houses. Setanta chased them down and with a swish of his stick felled stragglers as he went.

The king, who had been watching the amazing antics of the young lad, grabbed his wrist as he passed. "Stop little boy!" he ordered, "I see you do not play gently with the other lads. Why is that?"

"Master, I come from a faraway land and did not have an invitation to play," came the reply.

"Who are you then, boy?" demanded the king. "What is your name?"

"I am Setanta, master, the son of your very own sister."

A smile spread across the king's face. "Well then," he said, "tonight my men and I will feast at the house of Culann, a blacksmith from another village. You shall join me as my special guest."

"But master, I have travelled a great distance to play hurling and we have not finished our game yet!" exclaimed Setanta.

"You do not know where Culann lives. If you stay to finish your game, how will you find us?" pondered the king.

The boy boldly shot back a response; "I will follow the tracks of the horses and chariots."

"Very well," said King Conor, "we shall expect you in a while." With that, he left for the feast with a small band of his warriors while Setanta returned to the field and resumed his game with the other boys.

Later, as the air was filled with the shouts of mothers calling their young in for the evening, Setanta set off for the blacksmith's village, following the trail of footprints and tracks left by the king's party.

At the same time, a few miles to the south, King Conor and his men were arriving at the home of Culann the blacksmith.

"Welcome to my village Great Conor, I am honoured to have you as my guest!" bellowed the blacksmith. "Tell me, have you invited anyone else to join us?"

"No," replied the king, forgetting about Setanta, "it is just my men that you see around me. Why do you ask?"

"Sire, I own the most ferocious animal that Ireland has ever seen. It was given to me as a gift by sea-traders from Spain. Not only do I use it to herd cattle and sheep, but also to protect the village. When the sun goes down, I let the beast loose and no man will be allowed to enter."

"Set the animal to roam free," exclaimed the king, "and let us enjoy the feast you have prepared!"

Everyone followed the blacksmith into a great hall where a table laden with a mountain of the best food awaited. The hall was the size of ten houses with a high roof, held aloft by huge beams of oak. Hanging from the timbers were large iron baskets, filled with burning oil which sent flickering shadows to dance high above the revellers below.

At one end of the hall was a blazing hearth where twenty chefs, roasted pigs in the flames, while an army of children scurried back and forth, weighed down with trays of meat and jugs of wine to replenish the guests. Above all the laughing and shouting drifted the music of flutes and drums. The feast was in full swing!

By this time, Setanta was at the edge of the village and on hearing the festivities, had quickened his pace to a run.

Suddenly from the darkness came a blood-curdling howl, which stopped him dead in his tracks. Out of the shadows stalked the largest dog that he had ever seen. It looked as tall as a house, with fur the colour of a gathering storm, standing to attention all along its back. Bared teeth, long and sharp as daggers, glinted in the moonlight as the beast crept closer. All the while its eyes, like hot coals, burned through Setanta.

In an instant, the dog made a lunge. As quick as a flash, Setanta tossed up his silver ball and with a mighty swing of his hurley stick, it hurtled towards the horrific hound, making contact in mid-air. The impact sent the beast reeling backwards, head over tail like a tumbling ball of terror, until it was nearly out of sight. It rolled straight into a huge oak tree and with a last ear-splitting whine, fell dead.

Inside the hall, everyone heard the commotion and jumped up from their seats. The king, suddenly remembering that he had invited young Setanta to join them, feared the worst. "No good luck will come of this feast," he wailed, "I have let my own sister's son be undone by your hound!"

Throwing open the doors, every man rushed outside to see Setanta's fate. Fergus, the king's brother, was first to the scene where he found him standing over the limp body of the beast. Lifting the boy onto his shoulder, he brought him in front of King Conor.

It was the blacksmith's turn to cry. "What has happened? I am ruined! My friend is gone. Who will protect my village and my herds?"

From the shoulder of Fergus, Setanta bravely answered. "Do not be afraid, sir, I will find another dog of that breed from a good litter in Ireland, and I will train him for you. Until that day, I will protect you myself."

King Conor laughed and said to the blacksmith, "as king, I could not make you a better offer than the boy. From this day he shall be known as Cuchulainn, the Wolfhound of Culann!"

Cuchulainn protected the village and, in time, the whole of Ulster as he grew to be a mighty warrior.

This was due to a strange power that was unleashed when he got really angry.

A heated rage would turn him into a scary monster...

That's one hound who needed to be kept on a lead.

Once, an army of his friends got so scared that they threw him in a barrel of water to cool down.

...Such was the heat that the barrel exploded!

BOOOM

A second barrel boiled over and it was only a third that returned him to normal.

HISSSS

With this rage, Cuchulainn battled the enemies of Ulster, causing them trouble whenever they met.

What is a simile?

Make one up for this!

The jagged rocks were like...

Hidden beneath the countryside of Counties Fermanagh and Cavan, you will find the Marble Arch Caves.

Marble Arch Caves, County Fermanagh

These four hundred thousand year old caves are full of jagged rocks, or stalactites, that hang from the roof like ancient dragon teeth.

This underworld of rivers, waterfalls, winding passages and lofty chambers seems like it could be the gateway to a mysterious land!

Like the city under Lough Neagh?

Exactly Molly...and it's a place that one of the fiercest of Ulster chieftains was said to have been lured.

At a time when pagans battled over the misty, wild lands of Fermanagh, Donn Binn Maguire rode like the wind and fought with fury!

The great warrior took pride in galloping astride only the finest of horses.

So when the Maguire clan's bitter rivals, the O'Rourkes, claimed to have found the best horse in Ireland..

Donn Binn was furious and vowed to find the greatest horse in the world!

All to the interest of the Good People, who watched quietly from the shadows.

You see, the Good People live far beneath Ulster's surface and are forever trying to lure humans there.

As Donn Binn and his clansmen set off for the Fermanagh hills, where herds of horses ran free, the Good People hatched a plan.

These little folk are a magical race, and so, high on a misty mountain, they placed a beautiful enchanted stallion.

It took many hours of searching, but finally as the chieftain rode over a ridge, he stopped and gasped..

For grazing peacefully was the most perfect horse that had ever been seen!

...Except it wasn't seen, at least not by any of the other clansmen.

Unable to contain his excitement, the chieftain thundered towards the stallion...who bolted across the mountain.

While the rest of the confused party wondered what he was chasing!

The chieftain galloped hard, but never gained on the steed. Over rock, through bogs and streams and fields thick with heather he pursued.

Into a yawning cave, and down tunnels, which narrowed as they went deeper, until...

He burst into a mighty cavern, and pulled up on the shores of a vast lake that stretched into the darkness.

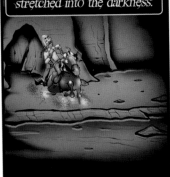

The white horse had vanished...and as he circled in confusion, he realised that the passageway was closing!

With Donn Binn trapped, the Good People emerged from the shadows to carry him across the lake to their kingdom.

30

Now, Donn Binn was treated well. He was fed with their finest food and serenaded with beautiful music played on magical pipes and harps.

On Ulster's surface, time moved on, years crept into centuries, but in the mysterious land, it meant nothing.

Away from the goodness of the sun, Donn Binn withered and paled, but he did not die.

Instead, he spent eternity dreaming of Fermanagh, of the people and the misty rolling landscapes that he once rode.

Seeing his misery, the Good People eventually took pity and granted him a special treat...

On certain nights, he would be allowed to roam the surface, but he must return to them... and bring another person!

So beware! The next time your family are gathered for an evening, be sure to draw the curtains...otherwise you might glance out the window to be met by a cold stare!

...And you'll know that Donn Binn has come to take someone back through the caves!

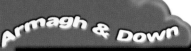

From Good People...

We're moving on to the story of a great man!

With two cathedrals, the city of Armagh is an important centre for Christianity in Ireland... and the ideal place to tell you about him.

City of Armagh

Armagh is close to Navan Fort, which, as we all know, is where a lot of pagans liked to hang out.

City of Armagh

The person who changed all that was born around 387AD, in Roman ruled Britain.

His name was Maewyn Succat and he was the son of a wealthy Roman tax collector.

Maewyn had a happy upbringing, until he was sixteen when a raiding party of Irish clansmen paid a visit.

...And collected the tax collector's son for the High King of Ireland... Niall of the Nine Hostages!

He was taken to Slemish Mountain in County Antrim and made to work as a shepherd.

To get through the loneliness and despair, Maewyn started talking to God.

Who talked back in a dream six years later!

He told Maewyn to escape and find passage home on a boat.

God wasn't finished and next He set the young man an important task.

To carry this out Maewyn first had to take another trip...this time to France.

Where he studied and trained in the Roman Catholic Church for the next fifteen years until...

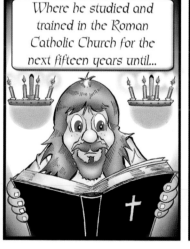

He emerged as a Bishop with a new name...from that day forth he would be known as Patrick!

Now he was ready for his mission...to convert the pagans of Ireland to Christianity!

33

Shamrock was sacred to pagans so, a story goes, Patrick used it when he was telling them about God.

In a shamrock there are three parts, and in God there are also three parts...The Father, The Son and The Holy Spirit.

Thanks to Patrick, the shamrock has become an important emblem of Ireland.

In the forty years that Patrick roamed the country, many tales were told about him.

Including one where he drove all the snakes out of Ireland!

He drove the snakes out of Ireland? What nonsense, they didn't even have cars back then!

PAT 1

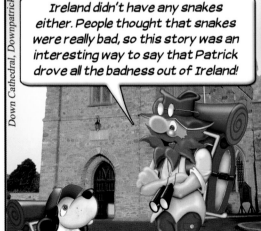

Down Cathedral, Downpatrick

Ireland didn't have any snakes either. People thought that snakes were really bad, so this story was an interesting way to say that Patrick drove all the badness out of Ireland!

Patrick died on 17th March 493AD. He's buried here at Down Cathedral.

Every year on that date, people all over the world celebrate Saint Patrick's Day!

Down Cathedral, Downpatrick

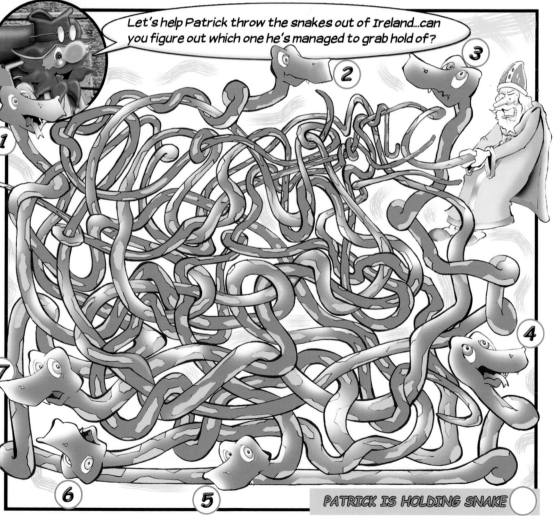

Let's help Patrick throw the snakes out of Ireland...can you figure out which one he's managed to grab hold of?

PATRICK IS HOLDING SNAKE

distance can be measured

in miles. Can you name any

other units that can be used

As Christianity grew, churches and monasteries popped up all over Ulster...and Saint Patrick's Trail is a good way to explore them.

Saint Patrick's Trail is a ninety-two mile route that leads to many sites relating to his legend, including Down Cathedral and Armagh.

Some of it also snakes around Strangford Lough, where he first landed on his mission to convert the pagans.

So when the pagan clans became Christian, did they all get along and live happily ever after?

Strangford Lough, County Down

Far from it Molly, many chieftains were still thirsty for power... and Strangford Lough is a handy place to tell you how far they would go to get it.

A myth goes that O'Neill, who was related to Niall of the Nine Hostages, was arguing with Dermott over who should be King of Ulster.

Surprisingly, rather than fight, they decided on a different way to settle the dispute...A BOAT RACE!

It was agreed that whoever charged across the Lough and touched land first would win.

...And with that win came the crown of Ulster!

With a mighty effort from their loyal clans, each chieftain battled for the lead as they swept across the water!

As land drew near, O'Neill turned to see an alarming sight.

Dermott had raced ahead and was only moments away from winning!

O'Neill realised that there was only one thing to do.

He chopped off his own hand and hurled it ashore!

Did that mean he touched land first and so became king?

Yes indeed, Molly.

They let someone that silly be king?

Not only that Max, many O'Neills became High King of Ireland over the following centuries.

...And the blood red hand sits proudly on the flag of Ulster!

After two hundred years of these raids, a bunch of Vikings settled in Normandy, which is in France.

Known as the Normans, they soon set their sights on England...and conquered it in 1066!

In 1169, the English Normans invaded Ireland. Their arrival signalled the end of the Irish High Kings.

...And the start of eight hundred years of trouble between the two countries.

If you love to learn about knights, then Carrickfergus Castle is a great place to visit.

IF1

After their invasion, Norman knights built castles like this to protect themselves from the Irish clans.

From its mighty walls they could rain rocks, arrows or even boiling oil down on any attackers.

Carrickfergus Castle, County Antrim

Of course, at first, the clans were too busy fighting each other to be of any threat.

This was until 1315, when an army of Scots, led by Edward Bruce, united enough of the clans to fight the English Normans.

At one point, Bruce laid siege to Carrickfergus Castle for over a year!

With no food or supplies getting to the Normans inside, they became hungry and desperate...

So hungry and desperate that they ate some prisoners from the castle dungeons!

Yuck! That's an Ulster Fry I wouldn't want to eat!

Now THAT one would be unhealthy!

Well, it was for the prisoners!

Carrickfergus Castle, County Antrim

In the end, Ireland turned out to be unhealthy for Edward Bruce...he was killed in battle three years later, allowing the English to continue their rule...

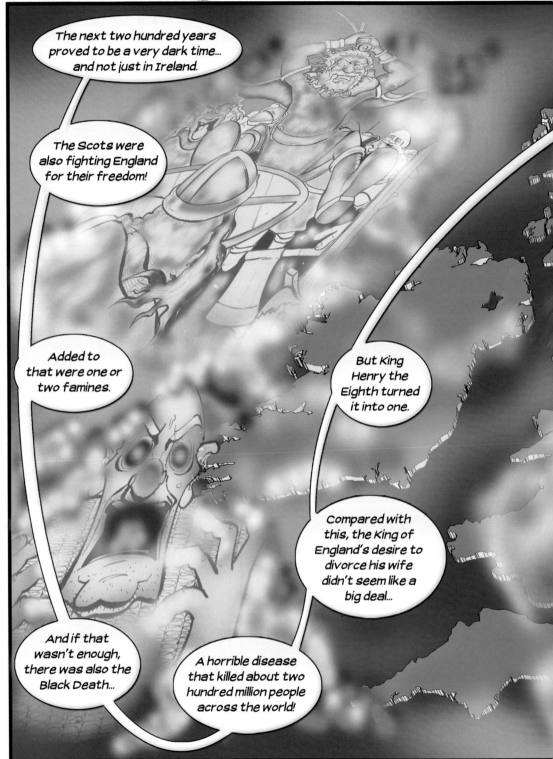

The next two hundred years proved to be a very dark time... and not just in Ireland.

The Scots were also fighting England for their freedom!

Added to that were one or two famines.

But King Henry the Eighth turned it into one.

Compared with this, the King of England's desire to divorce his wife didn't seem like a big deal...

And if that wasn't enough, there was also the Black Death...

A horrible disease that killed about two hundred million people across the world!

45

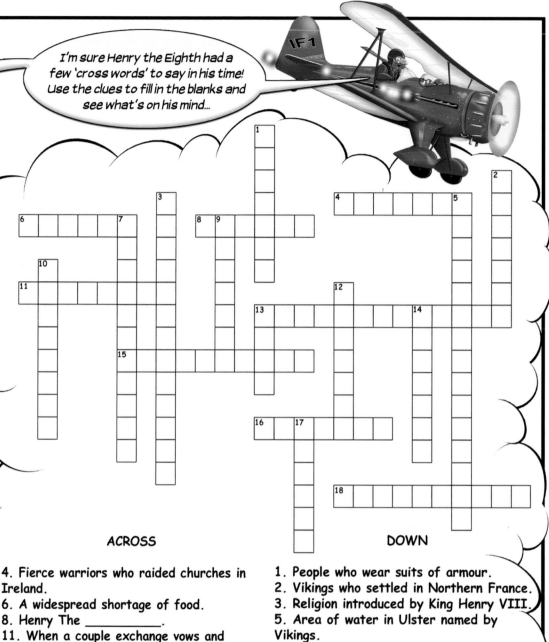

I'm sure Henry the Eighth had a few 'cross words' to say in his time! Use the clues to fill in the blanks and see what's on his mind...

ACROSS

4. Fierce warriors who raided churches in Ireland.
6. A widespread shortage of food.
8. Henry The _____.
11. When a couple exchange vows and rings.
13. Castle that was under siege for a year.
15. Disease that killed two hundred million people.
16. A place where prisoners in a castle were kept.
18. Poured from castle walls onto anyone who attacked.

DOWN

1. People who wear suits of armour.
2. Vikings who settled in Northern France.
3. Religion introduced by King Henry VIII.
5. Area of water in Ulster named by Vikings.
7. Scottish leader who fought the English.
9. Invaded by the Normans in 1169.
10. Church led by the Pope in Rome.
12. What King Henry VIII wanted from his wife.
13. A group that Irish warriors lived in.
14. Conquered by the Normans in 1066.
17. A country that the Vikings came from.

47

Imagine you found a bag of magic fairy dust. List the things you might do with it!

After all this talk of death, it would be good to visit a place where it doesn't exist.

IF1

...And here, in the stunning Glens of Antrim, is the perfect place to do that!

Glens of Antrim

With a little help from some magic!

FAIRY DUST

What we need is a fairy dust cloud to fly through.

Fairy dust?

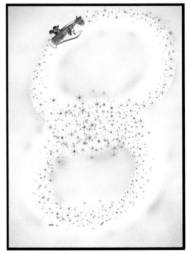

48

Glenariff Waterfall, Glens of Antrim

Far below Ireland's surface there exists a mysterious land.

This otherworld is a place where sickness and death do not roam.

It is the land of eternal youth and home to the Good People.

...Or to give them their more common name ...fairies!

The most famous kingdom in this otherworld is Tir Na Nog, which lies under the ocean, off Ireland's west coast.

Tir Na Nog is a paradise where fairies eat from cauldrons, which produce a never-ending supply of food.

It is very difficult for humans to travel here...but fairies can roam around our world at will.

...And the Glens of Antrim is a popular haunt!

All sorts of fairies make the trip, like the friendly grogoch who loves to work for humans in exchange for buckets of cream.

Although when you're a smelly fur ball, covered in dirt from your travels, it tends to send people running!

Of course, that most famous of fairies, the leprechaun, likes to spend his time hunting for gold.

While his cheeky cousin, the clurichaun, loves to cause mischief in people's houses.

Before swiping some things and escaping on a stolen chicken!

If there's one thing that fairies can't resist it's human babies.

Mostly because fairy babies look like little old monkeys who cry too much!

Given half the chance a fairy will take a human infant and leave theirs in its place!

They might even leave an old fairy...

Or a lump of wood!

With a sprinkling of fairy dust these replacements will look just like the original!

Although changelings, as they are known, will bring bad luck to the houses they are placed in!

Hawthorn tree

Speaking of bad luck, you should beware of hawthorn trees in the Glens of Antrim.

Locals refuse to cut them down because they are sacred to fairies.

Glens of Antrim

Those who do take an axe to them might find themselves cursed...

And end up with their heads on back to front!

Think I'll give those trees a miss!

If anyone does believe in these little folk, they should go to the east slope of Glencorp on April 30th.

...Because it's said that every year fairies have their very own parade!

Let's go on a hunt for fairies! See if you can spot it, along with these other fairy related phrases in the word search below.

FAIRIES   GLENS OF ANTRIM   ULSTER   TIR NA NOG   LEPRECHAUN
CLURICHAUN   GROGOCH   CHANGELING   BANSHEE   LITTLE FOLK
GOOD PEOPLE   HAWTHORN TREE   GLENCORP   IRELAND

```
A H J K B N Q M S D L O O F P R S K N I R E L A N D G I E
S B A N S H E E I S R T B M H C R E T S L U P O E N U O H
T T U S V O O M W X U Y S Y N W Q S U P O D M U U T L O S
G L E N S O F A N T R I M N C J Y R A Q P V X H F Y S H O
U R S E Y M Q I A K C M T A A G S D E R N M Y G I M V W D
M G V U O T W Q U S E U E U G L W B W X T U E A U W Q R S
D A F L T U Y M H A M Y Q S R C H A N G E L I N G C H M N
U N J Y Q S R A I Z R V U J O R W Y U W R Z Q O W S Y E U
W O X W L W L I Q Y R Z B Y G Y S X P C Q Y X O Z Y C T T
E Y B U D M Y H G H Z X Y S O K D B S I H L B Y W F Y W J
X L Q K X I S A P S H R A D C A N D V Y R U M M Z Y X S O
J L D O V H P M Y C A T U O H L X F M Q Y S T I L Y K E V
F I M X M T X Q S F W D P P E M U L F F G R T A O N D Y E
V O I B V F W D Z U T Y D K R P X T R B N W Y X I J S A H
L N O S N P T O X A H D G T R T A C X A B P Y V M N F X E
R J U K W R X Y B E O G I O A L M S V K W N A U Q O N T L
N N A J D E T W Q Z R T W X X G L E N C O R P Z J S X A I
U M O S J C I H W A N Q C I R C N Z X H W C E R H A Q L T
A L U T V W R S P P T H J K A F J E V V Y S N J D V X O T
H F X G S Y N F X G R S H A V W V T C T Q Y U M S G B W L
C J K V I N A A M H E D Z R S U X F F S G S A I N L Z Y E
I H O S A I N Q I L E V T M V A G G M V I S H E S T X X F
R Z B F W D O P Y I P N Y D Q R W H T T J X C B U Z V J O
U V L L K O G Y Z A B A P X Q S Z E F K N Y E V Y U C W L
L E J D N X Y Q N T S U Q Y X Z L O O B C M R N I F K O K
C O E W A G O O D P E O P L E L A H G D O W P L X B A H U
U U F Y C V W E A A C N B X F G E F Q C Y L E W V B O J D
S E I R I A F C H K R E Q G S L O A M S U P L D N T F W Z
```

Dunluce Castle

An acrostic poem for 'CLAN'...

Celtic warriors Led by chieftains

A Norman attacking Norman castle

pick a word and write your own!

Sitting on the Antrim Coast is another old Norman fortress...Dunluce Castle!

Dunluce Castle, County Antrim

Down through the ages, the English fought clans, and the clans fought each other for control of it.

Dunluce Castle, County Antrim

Today though, the only thing said to be living in it is a banshee.

What's a banshee?

A banshee is another kind of fairy. Supposedly it's the spirit of a woman.

This one is called Maeve and she spends eternity sweeping her room!

Now, there's one thing you should know about banshees...

54

Huge waves crashed constantly against ragged rocks at the base of a sheer cliff, as high above Dunluce Castle stood, peering over the edge at this never-ending battle.

The scene was home to another battler, a fierce chieftain named McQuillan, who lived in the castle with his beautiful daughter Maeve. McQuillan was an ambitious man and although he cherished the girl, his heart warmed just as much for power and position. This, he believed, could be strengthened if Maeve married another chieftain, Roy Oge, bringing two mighty clans together.

However, when McQuillan introduced the pair and suggested a union, Maeve was horrified and fled in tears to her room. The chieftain was embarrassed for Roy Oge and furious at his daughter's behaviour. Why would she act in such a foolish manner?

The answer was that Maeve was in love with another. Not just anybody, but Reg O'Cahan, McQuillan's bitter enemy! She had fallen for the dashing young man months earlier, when he was imprisoned in the castle tower.

Roy Oge was shrewd and suspected that a rival stood in his way. Employing spies, he soon learned that Maeve and O'Cahan regularly met in secret under the 'Wishing Arch', a short distance along the coast.

When this news was reported to McQuillan, the enraged chieftain hurled the girl into her room, vowing that she wouldn't leave unless she agreed to marry Roy Oge. As he locked the door, Maeve screamed that she would rather die than marry a man she did not love!

Days later, when McQuillan finally returned, Maeve was sewing a white garment. The chieftain was overjoyed.

"Ah, your wedding gown!" he beamed.

"No, my funeral shroud!" she stubbornly replied.

Twice more this happened and on the third occasion Maeve's father snapped. Grabbing a broom, he threw it at her, yelling, "sweep your own room! If you don't want to marry and become a lady of honour, then I shall allow no servants to attend you!"

A further week passed and on his next visit McQuillan was surprised to find the room swept clean and thought all must be well.

"So, your bridal gown is ready?" he enquired.

"No, but my funeral shroud is," was the reply from his brooding daughter as she picked up the broom and started to sweep some more.

The words fell heavy. Despite his disappointment that she had fallen for his sworn enemy, McQuillan truly loved his daughter and despaired at seeing her so sad and wretched. At that moment the chieftain realised what he must do.

Unbeknown to Maeve, he devised a plan that would allow her to be with the man she loved without the loss of any dignity for himself. Word was sent to O'Cahan that one evening the chieftain would be away and Maeve's door would be left unlocked.

As the evening arrived, Maeve was feeling particularly sad and had dressed in the white shroud, pining for her lost love. As she stared from the window, she was horrified to spot her father setting out from the castle accompanied by a formidable raiding party of his loyal soldiers. As their horses disappeared over the hills, Maeve was convinced that her father had finally decided to rid the world of her beloved Reg.

Just then, her bedroom door eased open and a low voice whispered, "My lady, follow me. O'Cahan waits in a cave below the castle."

In an instant, Maeve was hurrying after the mysterious figure, down to the vast cavern where she found Reg waiting with a boat. After a hasty embrace they cast off for a life of freedom together!

The night sky, however, masked a gathering storm and the pair struggled as the waters grew angry. By this time McQuillan had returned to check that his plan had worked and, from the castle, he could just make out Maeve's white figure through the spray of the breaking waves. Realising they were in distress, he frantically ordered his own boat to the rescue and offered half of all his possessions to the man who would save his daughter.

McQuillan's best warriors rowed for all they were worth but the raging sea battered them backwards. The rescue attempt was hopeless.

The next morning O'Cahan's body washed up on the shore but Maeve was never to be seen again. To this day though, her room in the castle is still mysteriously swept clean...

What a sad story.

Speaking of boats, the Armada sailed past here in 1588.

Dunluce Castle, County Antrim

The Armada was a fleet of one hundred and thirty ships, sent by the Catholic King of Spain to attack England and stop the rise of Protestantism...but it failed!

As the Spanish made their escape, they were hit by bad weather and many ships perished along the Irish coast.

One called The Girona sank near Dunluce Castle.

58

What is an adverb?

Add 1 to this sentence:

Molly, Max and Mick

Molly has been scared speechless by the banshee story. Can you match the captions to the correct pictures and find out what happened next in Ulster?

The Protestant settlers built walls around this city to protect them from attack by the Catholic Irish. They named it Londonderry.

This sculpture in Donegal depicts some chieftains fleeing from Ulster in 1607, following a nine year war with the English. This event was known as 'The Flight of the Earls'.

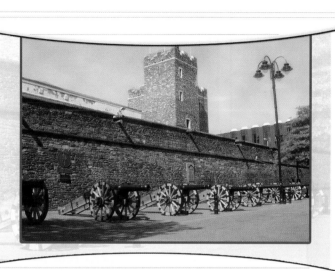

'Roaring Meg' was the name of a cannon used during 'The Siege of Derry' in 1690, when some Protestants defended the city against an army of Catholics.

Springhill House was built during 'The Plantation of Ulster', a plan by the English to move Protestants into the province.

61

Get some tape or glue

and lots of lollipop sticks!

If you scare easily, then you probably shouldn't try to cross the Carrick-a-Rede Rope Bridge.

For over three hundred and fifty years fishermen on the Antrim Coast crossed this gap to get to the tiny Carrick Island where they would catch the passing salmon.

Carrick-a-Rede Rope Bridge, County Antrim

Do you think that you could cross the Carrick-a-Rede Rope Bridge Max?

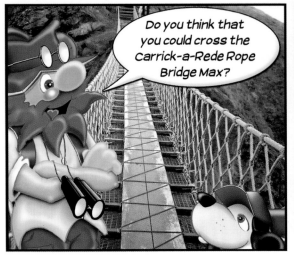

Cross it? I can't even spell it!

Carrick-a-Rede Rope Bridge, County Antrim

Let's play the bridge quiz!
Answer the questions and see if you can get
Max all the way to the other side!

What **C** was a tribe who came to Ireland in 600BC?

What **A** has Glens full of fairies?

What **R** is the colour of the hand on the Ulster flag?

What **R** ruled Britain in Maewyn Succat's time?

What **I** did Finn create in the Irish Sea?

What **C** was Setanta renamed?

What **K** was Henry The Eighth?

What **A** was The Girona part of?

What **R** is a Siege of Derry cannon?

What **E** was Navan Fort known as?

What **D** is Maeve's castle?

What **E** took flight from Donegal in 1607?

63

You know, if you pay a visit to the Ulster American Folk Park in County Tyrone, you'll be able to travel back to this period as well!

At the Folk Park, you'll see how The Great Hunger was one reason why millions left their homes in Ireland.

© Ulster American Folk Park, Omagh

They travelled great distances, over sea and land to make a new life in America!

© Ulster American Folk Park, Omagh

The brave Ulster folk who made this trip helped to shape a new nation.

© Ulster American Folk Park, Omagh

As we return to our time, here's a chance for you to be a detective.

All of these men came from families who emigrated from Ulster. Can you use your research skills to investigate who they were?

John Dunlap
Andrew Jackson
James Buchanan
Davy Crockett
Chester Arthur

65

66

69

Titanic's 20 life-boats held

about 1200 people. How many

could each lifeboat take?

The shipyard, started by a Mr. Harland and a Mr. Wolff, also built Titanic.

One of the main German targets was a shipyard, which was building vessels for the British Royal Navy.

Harland and Wolff Shipyard, Belfast

Mr. Wolf? I thought he spent his time chasing the three little pigs!

Or was it Little Red Riding Hood?

What time is it Mr Wolf?

IT'S SHIPBUILDING TIME!

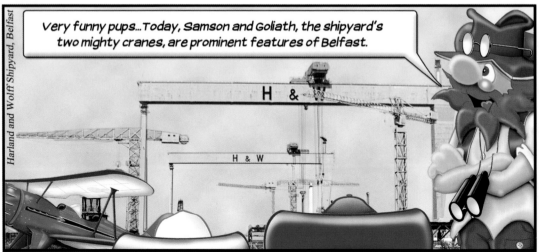

Very funny pups...Today, Samson and Goliath, the shipyard's two mighty cranes, are prominent features of Belfast.

Harland and Wolff Shipyard, Belfast

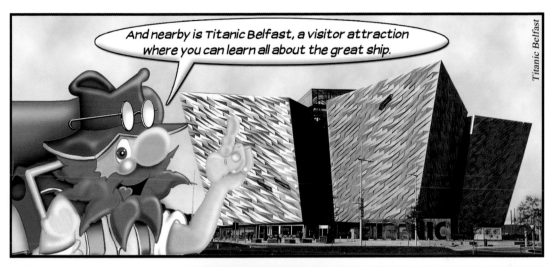

Titanic Belfast

As well as finding out all about her fateful voyage.

That looks amazing!

Outside, you can board the SS Nomadic, which was used to ferry passengers to Titanic all those years ago.

SS Nomadic, Belfast

While seven miles away, in Holywood...

Hollywood... isn't that where they make movies?

Did they make the Titanic movie there?

there were about 2200 people *aboard Titanic. How many* *more lifeboats should* *she have carried?*

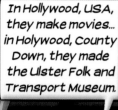

In Hollywood, USA, they make movies... in Holywood, County Down, they made the Ulster Folk and Transport Museum.

You can spend a wonderful day here exploring life in Ulster around Titanic's time.

© Ulster Folk and Transport Museum, County Down

...And seeing lots of vehicles from Ulster's past.

You could make a Thomas the Tank Engine movie here!

© Ulster Folk and Transport Museum, County Down

There's also a fantastic Titanica Exhibition.

If we can't watch a movie, can you tell us a story about Titanic?

Hmm, let me think...

© Ulster Folk and Transport Museum, County Down

Sunlight twinkled on the calm waters of Belfast Lough and draped itself across the rows of tiny red-bricked houses that huddled nearby, as dawn broke over the city. The old one-armed sailor paused to bask in its warmth, closing his eyes and savouring the peace. Then, with a mighty roar, he shattered the silence.

"GET UP!"

Hobbling from house to house, he clattered a stick against windows and doors, for it was his job to wake the workers inside. Of course, Sam was already up. When you lived rough, sleep was as elusive as the rats that shared the streets. There was always a bed in the workhouse, but that place was crammed with other orphans, all wailing in the night for parents who would never come. It was a living nightmare that Sam had to escape.

The youngster spent these early mornings at the gates of Harland and Wolff Shipyard. Looking up at its huge gantries, which loomed over the cobbled streets like giant climbing frames, always brightened the spirits. These gantries held ships upright as they were built and standing there now was the one they called RMS Titanic. It was said that Titanic would take just six days to cross the Atlantic Ocean to America, a land of plenty, where dreams could come true. Sam's dream was to travel there on board that majestic vessel.

As the orphan's mind drifted across the ocean to that new world, the earliest workers trickled onto the streets. Not long after, the floodgates opened and fifteen thousand men surged towards the shipyard. They washed past the scruffy little urchin, before fanning out to take up their stations beyond the iron gates.

Suddenly, a whistle shrilled, signalling the start of the six o'clock shift. As echoes rebounded along narrow streets, Sam stared awestruck as four thousand men clambered like ants over the scaffolding that surrounded Titanic. A cacophony of noise exploded as steam cranes rumbled on rails, hoisting huge sheets of thick steel. Furnaces roared and the clangs of heavy hammers rang out like church bells...the famous Belfast symphony was in full swing!

It was 31st March 1909 when Titanic's keel, the spine of the ship, was laid. Over the following year, Sam had seen her skeleton slowly rise. As the summer of 1910 drifted towards autumn, her skin had been grafted on. Three million red-hot rivets were hammered into the steel panels, fixing them in place and making Titanic's hull, the ship's body, completely watertight.

Life on the street was even more of a struggle when winter closed in. The only thing that warmed Sam on those cold, dark nights was the sight of Titanic. Thoughts of sailing away on her swathed the child like a blanket.

That day seemed much closer on 31st May 1911. At noon, a red rocket lit up the sky over Belfast. Excitement fizzled as Sam joined one hundred thousand others to see Titanic's launch. Fifteen minutes later, a second rocket exploded and the heaviest object ever moved by man took just a minute to slide down the greasy slipway into Belfast Lough.

Although floating, it would be a further ten months before Titanic was ready. While her boilers, engines and propellers were being installed, she was also painted. Inside the ship, tiles and carpets were laid and crystal chandeliers hung. There were rich white columns and beautifully moulded ceilings. Oak, cut from Tollymore Forest, at the foot of the Mourne Mountains, was used to carve staircases, panelling and furniture for the upper decks.

When twenty horses hauled one of the ship's immense anchors, on a wagon through the streets of Belfast, Sam realised that she was almost complete. When the last of the four huge funnels was hoisted into place and Titanic sat proudly as the greatest passenger liner ever built, Sam knew it was time to act. It was time to sneak on board.

Rain drizzled down on the morning of 31st March 1912 when the last of the wagons from Kelly's Coal Yard arrived at Harland and Wolff. Titanic's sea trials were scheduled for the following day and her fuel was still being loaded. As the Belfast symphony rang out, one of the wagon horses startled. Coal men and shipyard workers rushed to control her. In that moment of chaos, Sam leapt onto the wagon and slid between some wet coal bags.

When the horse was finally calmed, it was eased through the gates, hauling the wagon behind her.

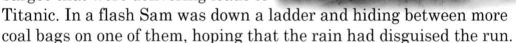

Minutes later, just as the heavens opened, the wagon came to a halt. On board, a small pair of eyes squinted through lashing rain, to see that they stood at the edge of a dock. Below them sat little coal barges that were delivering loads to Titanic. In a flash Sam was down a ladder and hiding between more coal bags on one of them, hoping that the rain had disguised the run.

The barge swayed, but time seemed to stand still. Sam's heart beat like a bass drum through those frozen moments. Then, with a mumble of voices and the rumble of an engine, the vessel spluttered into life.

"Get alongside the coal port," yelled a crewman.

The little barge rolled to and fro in the choppy water as they drew ever closer to Titanic. When they met for the first time, like a goldfish nuzzling a whale, Sam sprang into action; diving through the hatch in the ship's belly, crashing onto a heap of coal, then scrambling to the shadows to pray that no one had noticed.

Seconds turned to minutes, which blended into hours, but nobody came. Throughout the morning coal clattered down causing dusty, black avalanches in the bunker. Still nobody came. When the coal port was sealed and only silence fell, nobody was going to. Sam was all alone...except for the two grimy figures that crouched quietly nearby.

Huddled in a corner, with knees hugged to fight off the cold, Sam heard a tiny cough tickle the air and froze instantly. It happened again, then half another. Like someone small, a child perhaps, was trying to stifle it. The cough escaped, heaved out by four more.

"Shhh," came a whisper as the coughs turned to hacks and splutters. "Shhh," repeated the voice, "ya'll get yerself catched!"

In a panic Sam lashed out at the darkness and grabbed what felt like a tiny collar.

"Grand! Wha' did I tell ye? Ya've gone an' got yerself nabbed...ya eejit!" spat the voice.

"I couldn't help it, there's too much dust in here," choked a response from Sam's clasped hand. There seemed to be a small shadow madly wriggling to escape. From out of nowhere another grubby little figure appeared with arms flailing wildly at its partner.

"Grand work, now we has ta grant dis huey-man tree wishies!"

"What are you?" asked Sam.

"Wha' are we?" it responded, "we's Good People a-course!"

"Though ye may know us as leprechauns," added the other, "I'm Argal and that's Shmee."

"'Aving a wee kip up a great oak tree in tha' forest ye call Tollymore. Minding our own busy-ness, when some huey-mans comed and cutted 'er down!" continued Shmee, "dragged it away ta be used in dis ship!"

"So do you want to travel to America, like me?" asked Sam.

"Mer Ca? Mer Ca? Who cares 'bout Mer Ca? We've been 'earing all the natter 'bout Tanic. Bestest ship ever built. Which means she'll be packed full a-rich huey-mans! Which means she'll be full a-glimmer!" giggled Shmee, rubbing his hands with glee.

"He means gold," Argal said, "Watches, rings, necklaces..."

"Get our 'ands on tha' glimmer and we'll be tha' richest folk in Tir Na Nog!" roared Shmee before breaking into a merry little jig.

"Anyway, Shmee was right, ye caught me and now I owe ya three wishes," said Argal.

Sam was taken aback, "I get three wishes?"

"Aye," said Shmee, "and can ye 'urry, so we can look fer glimmer!"

Sam sat in a state of disbelief. Was this really happening? There was only one way to find out. With eyes closed tight, the child gulped a breath, "I want to go to America."

"Wha' is dis Mer Ca ya keep slabberin' 'bout?" demanded Shmee.

"It's a land of plenty, to the west of Ireland, where I will be happy," Sam replied.

"Ok," said Argal, "but don't say want, ya have to wish for it."

With eyes clasped shut, Sam spoke slowly, "I wish to go to that land of plenty...the land to the west of Ireland."

Suddenly, the ship sailed into the child's mind, all those months of watching it grow. A smile spread from ear to ear, "but first I wish I could explore Titanic!"

Argal clicked his fingers and struck a spark of brilliant blue.

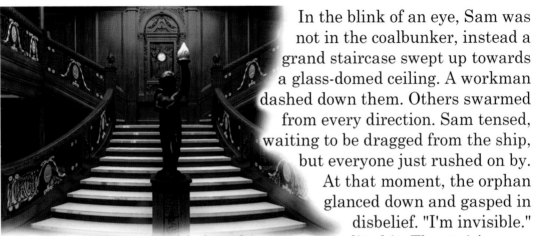

In the blink of an eye, Sam was not in the coalbunker, instead a grand staircase swept up towards a glass-domed ceiling. A workman dashed down them. Others swarmed from every direction. Sam tensed, waiting to be dragged from the ship, but everyone just rushed on by. At that moment, the orphan glanced down and gasped in disbelief. "I'm invisible."

Sam's legs almost buckled as this strange reality hit. The stair's bannister provided some support, allowing the child to creep upwards, past a beautifully carved clock and on to the boat deck. There, a view of Belfast sprawled into the distance. Although it was early evening, the shipyard was still bustling in preparation for the next morning's sea trials. Until then though, the ship was Sam's to explore.

Titanic was a feast for the senses. Everything smelt new; fresh paint, varnish, polish and floor wax. There was fine linen and oak carvings to be caressed. The sensation of an electric elevator magically whizzing from Deck A to Deck E. Bread from the kitchens to be eaten while strolling through the majestic 'Jacobean Room', the first class dining hall, as grand as anything the finest of hotels could offer.

Titanic dripped with extravagance. It was the first ship to have a swimming pool, Turkish baths, squash courts and a gym! Finally, when exhaustion overcame curiosity, the child curled up on a bed inside an exquisite first class cabin and fell asleep.

As morning drew in, so too did the storm clouds. Howling wind and lashing rain battered the port, delaying Titanic's trials by a day. Sam spent the time exploring parts of Titanic that stretched below water. Down there were sixteen compartments that ran the length of her. If one of these flooded, it could be sealed, making her almost unsinkable.

At first light on Tuesday 2nd April 1912, Titanic was hauled down Belfast Lough as crowds of well-wishers waved from the shore. Hercules, Harland and Wolff's stocky little tugboat led the team of vessels that dragged her. Two miles off the coast, they dropped their ropes and Titanic was unleashed.

With blood boiling in excitement, Sam paced the foredeck, staring out at Carrickfergus Castle, which loomed in the distance. Far below, the crew stoked boilers and released valves, allowing steam to race towards the two mighty engines. The propellers groaned, as if letting out an almighty yawn, and then began to turn. Slowly, the giant awoke from its slumber and began to crawl through the water.

Wind battered Sam's face as Titanic surged forward, fully alert now and eager for the run. Suddenly, her engines were cut and she was allowed to drift. This was only one of many tests that she would be put through. All day she would stop and start, travel in straight lines and circles, twist port, then starboard and drop anchor. Finally, at seven o'clock in the evening, RMS Titanic was passed fit for sea and she bade farewell to Belfast forever.

White Star Line, the company that owned Titanic, had chosen Southampton on the south coast of England as the starting point for her voyages. With London nearby, the ship would have a roaring trade. For three whole days Sam watched as Titanic's stores were loaded with provisions to feed more than two thousand passengers and crew. The potatoes alone were the weight of ten elephants!

On Wednesday 10th April 1912, most of the passengers and crew joined the ship, cheerful and ready to begin their momentous journey. Captain Smith cut a noble figure as he arrived on the pier, ready to take command of Titanic. With a beard as white as wisps of water that trailed in a ship's wake, he looked every inch the brave seaman. Thomas Andrews, who designed the vessel, along with Bruce Ismay, the chairman of White Star Line greeted him as Sam flitted nearby, feeling that greatness was within touching distance.

Just after midday, Titanic set sail to the cheers of the crowds who lined the quayside. Traversing the English Channel, she berthed briefly at Cherbourg, in France, and Queenstown, on Ireland's south coast, to pick up more passengers. Then, with all twenty-nine of her boilers fully stoked, she set off for Pier 59 in New York City.

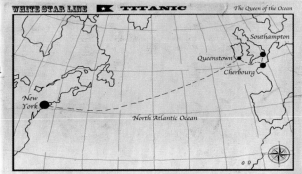

Cloaked with the gift of invisibility, Sam ghosted through First Class, where the well to do roamed; watching Lords and Ladies mingle with important business people like Benjamin Guggenheim and the richest man in the world, JJ Astor. Wondering if Argal and Shmee were watching them too, as they hunted for gold.

Like a gentle breeze, the orphan swirled unnoticed around Cafe Parisien, scanning the long ivy-clad room for the leprechauns as they picked pockets. Quick peeks under tables and chairs revealed nothing, but a peer out of a window did. A familiar young face stained with hardship and eyes as blue as the ocean beyond, stared back.

Suddenly, a scream pierced the polite conversation, causing a fearful frown to sear its way across the face. Sam's face, reflecting in the glass and exposed for all to see. Argal's spell had worn off.

"ARGHHHH!" shrieked an older lady who pointed in horror. Before her a startled, young tearaway stood. Waves of shock swept through the room as other diners craned their necks and stared, their eyes as wide as their soup bowls. The rising gasps rolled into a crescendo of chaotic noise that tumbled and splashed a cold realisation over the child. Flee the scene or feel the fury of Titanic's crew.

With a mind swimming in fear, Sam bolted from Cafe Parisien; straight to the Grand Staircase, descending from Deck B to Deck E where all fineries were stripped away. Plain steps led down deeper to Decks F and G, where it would be easier to blend in with the third class passengers. Poor migrants, who like Sam, dreamt of a better life in America. Little did they know that most would never make it.

Just before midnight on Sunday 14th April, Sam was amongst a crowd in the dining saloon, when they felt a grinding shudder. Soon, whispers began to spread that they had hit an iceberg. Over the next two hours, voices grew louder as the ship began to slowly tilt. When seawater started to seep down corridors, panic set in. Rushing for stairwells, they found their escape blocked by iron gates. Suddenly the ship let out a painful groan. A wave of dread was chased by a wave of water that rounded a corner and smashed into them.

Twisting and twirling in the wash, eyes bulging, begging for breath, Sam wished there was a way to escape this horror. Suddenly the briefest pulse of hope penetrated the intense pain. Three wishes. Two had been used. There was one left.

"I wish that I was out of this ship!" mouthed Sam, choking on water.

Coughs and gags were replaced with gasps for the cool sweet air that was instantly all around. As the lung-bursting agony subsided, Sam looked up to a majestic sky pinpricked with stars marching through the heavens. Then the cold bit again. Mirroring the sky was the ocean, seemingly connected by Titanic, which stood upright like a tower. All around were shrieking passengers who flapped and thrashed in the water, while lifeboats floated helplessly in the distance. Sam was out of the ship, but not out of danger.

Slowly, the great vessel began to slide into the steely death-blackness of the Atlantic, pulling Sam down too. Dragged ever deeper, a final breath burst free in a jet of dancing bubbles, taking all terror with it. Hugged by a warmth that was strangely comforting, Sam faded into darkness glimpsing two tiny figures on the way.

"Must be the angels guiding me to heaven," a reassuring voice from within whispered, as eternal night fell.

"WAKE UP!"

Sam's eyes flickered open. There was no choking water, no struggle to breath and no biting cold. Instead there was soft grass all around. Flowers of the most striking colours stood swaying in a warm breeze. Also standing there were Argal and Shmee.

"Where am I?" croaked Sam.

"In the land o' plenty, to the West of Ireland," replied Argal, "just like ya wished for!"

Sam's eyes shone like the moon, "America?"

"Mer Ca, Mer Ca, Mer Ca!" shouted Shmee, "'Ere we go 'gain 'bout Mer Ca!"

The little leprechaun hopped up and down, "Yer not in Mer Ca," he said, before spreading his arms out wide. "Yer in our land a-plenty, the land a-tha fairies!"

"...Where there's no death, no sickness and no hunger," continued Argal. "Yer in Tir Na Nog. Welcome!"

In Titanic's time, radios could not transmit voices, just clicking noises. A short click was called a dot while a longer one was a dash. Using this system, ships could talk to each other using Morse code.

INTERNATIONAL MORSE CODE

A	• —		U	• • —
B	— • • •		V	• • • —
C	— • — •		W	• — —
D	— • •		X	— • • —
E	•		Y	— • — —
F	• • — •		Z	— — • •
G	— — •			
H	• • • •			
I	• •			
J	• — — —		1	• — — — —
K	— • —		2	• • — — —
L	• — • •		3	• • • — —
M	— —		4	• • • • —
N	— •		5	• • • • •
O	— — —		6	— • • • •
P	• — — •		7	— — • • •
Q	— — • —		8	— — — • •
R	• — •		9	— — — — •
S	• • •		0	— — — — —
T	—			

For example, after hitting the iceberg, Titanic crewmen signalled for help from other ships. They sent out three short clicks, or dots, followed by three longer ones, or dashes, followed by another three short ones.

S   O   S

Their message was 'SOS', which is a well-known distress call...some people say that it means 'Save Our Ship' or 'Save Our Souls'.

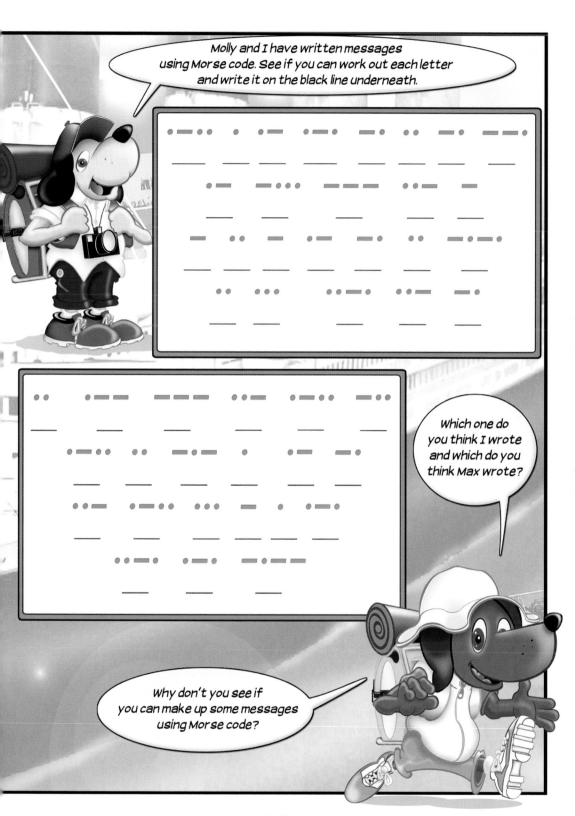

© Ulster Museum, Belfast

We're continuing our trip by exploring the Ulster Museum. With its cool layout, you could lose yourself in the history for hours!

Which reminds me, can you spot Max and Molly wandering somewhere below?

85

Many Irish people didn't want this...

They wanted to break away and rule themselves.

Scotland

Ireland

England

Wales

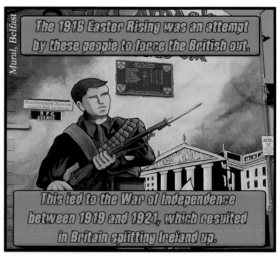

Mural, Belfast

The 1916 Easter Rising was an attempt by these people to force the British out.

This led to the War of Independence between 1919 and 1921, which resulted in Britain splitting Ireland up.

Northern Ireland's mainly Protestant population wanted to stay British.

While the Republic of Ireland was set up for the mainly Catholic population.

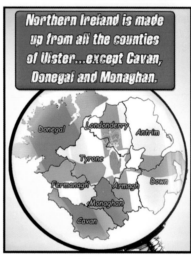

Northern Ireland is made up from all the counties of Ulster...except Cavan, Donegal and Monaghan.

Donegal

Londonderry

Antrim

Tyrone

Fermanagh

Armagh

Down

Monaghan

Cavan

Hold on, I'm confused, are we in Northern Ireland or Ulster?

If you think it's confusing now, it was much worse during the Troubles!

Some people wanted Northern Ireland to join the Republic and in 1969, violence erupted, which lasted for thirty years!

Mural, Belfast

Finally, in 1998, politicians from all sides put their heads together...

And came up with a way that everyone could live in peace...It was called the Good Friday Agreement.

86

ANSWERS

The Lands of C.S Lewis

Turn these 6P's into a story!

Imagine you find a 'Place'.

A sec land wi populat.

When CS Lewis looked upon parts of his native land, he didn't see Ulster or Northern Ireland.

...And it inspired him to write a book. See if you can guess what it is called!

'The Searcher', a statue on the Holywood Road in Belfast, close to the author's birthplace, shows him about to climb into a wardrobe.

Where a land full of mythical creatures awaited! Lewis likened this land to the rugged Mourne Mountains in County Down.

He wrote of how this land had been cursed by an evil white witch who made it 'always winter but never Christmas!'

The kings and queens who oppose the witch have their thrones at Cair Paravel...a castle not unlike the one at Dunluce.

Ulster people have a long tradition of painting murals. Here's one of Aslan the Lion in the mysterious land...a land that Lewis named Narnia!

Great, now I don't know if I'm in Ulster or Narnia!

90

1941

1169

795AD

387AD

600BC
THE CELTS ARRIVE

1588

  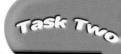

TABLE A

ANIMAL	ADJECTIVES TO DESCRIBE IT	MOVEMENT VERB
Example Snake	Long, scaly, poisonous	Slithers

TABLE B

ACTION OF CHIMP	TALLY
Sits down	
Eats	
Climbs	
Runs	
Calls out	
Grooms a friend	

TABLE C

ANIMAL	NATURAL HABITAT	REASON IT IS ENDANGERED
Example Panda	Bamboo forests, China	Destruction of habitat

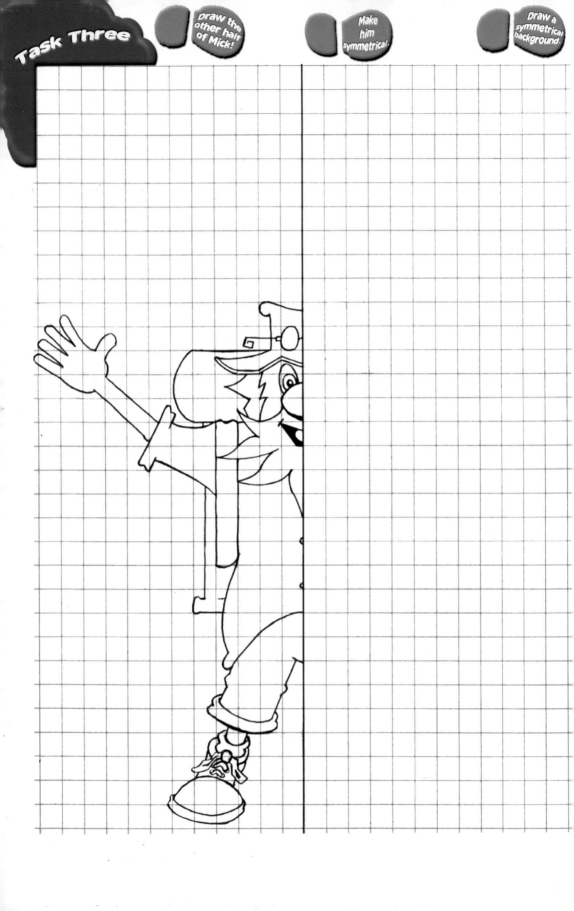

Task Three

draw the other half of Mick!

Make him symmetrical.

draw a symmetrical background.